REPTILES

Izzi Howell

WAYLAND
www.waylandbooks.co.uk

FACT CAT

Get your paws on this fantastic new mega-series from Wayland!

Join our Fact Cat on a journey of fun learning about every subject under the sun!

First published in Great Britain in 2015 by Wayland
Copyright © Wayland 2015

ISBN: 978 0 7502 9602 1
Dewey Number: 597.9-dc23
10 9 8 7 6 5 4 3 2 1

MIX
Paper from responsible sources
FSC® C104740

Wayland
An imprint of Hachette Children's Group
Part of Hodder & Stoughton
Carmelite House
50 Victoria Embankment
London EC4Y 0DZ

An Hachette UK Company
www.hachette.co.uk
www.hachettechildrens.co.uk

A catalogue for this title is available from the British Library
Printed and bound in China

Produced for Wayland by
White-Thomson Publishing Ltd
www.wtpub.co.uk

Editor: Izzi Howell
Design: Clare Nicholas
Fact Cat illustrations: Shutterstock/Julien Troneur
Other illustrations: Stefan Chabluk
Consultant: Kate Ruttle

Picture and illustration credits:
Corbis: Paul Souders 12, Bence Mate/Nature Picture Library 20; iStock: CathyKeifer 4bl, astra490 16, FourOaks 18; Shutterstock: Aleksey Stemmer cover, Maciej Wlodarczyk title page and 6, paytai 4 tl, Raffaella Calzoni 4tr, Achimdiver 4br, Gudkov Andrey 5, ShaunWilkinson 7, tharamust 8, defpicture 9l, Rich Carey 9r, Janelle Lugge 10t, Yellowj 10b, Karel Gallas 11, Gumpanat 13, Paul Tessier 14, beltsazar 15, Ery Azmeer 17, Chantelle Bosch 19, Ian Kennedy 21.

Every effort has been made to clear copyright.
Should there be any inadvertent omission,
please apply to the publisher for rectification.

The author, Izzi Howell, is a writer and editor specialising in children's educational publishing.

The consultant, Kate Ruttle, is a literacy expert and SENCO, and teaches in Suffolk.

FACT CAT FACT

There is a question for you to answer on each spread in this book. You can check your answers on page 24.

CONTENTS

What is a reptile? 4

Habitats 6

Breathing 8

Scales and shells.............. 10

Diet 12

Young......................... 14

Movement...................... 16

Senses 18

Strange reptiles 20

Quiz......................... 22

Glossary...................... 23

Index......................... 24

Answers....................... 24

WHAT IS A REPTILE?

Reptiles are a group of animals that are similar to each other in certain ways. Most reptiles are covered in **scales**, instead of skin or **fur**. Almost all reptiles lay eggs although a few give birth to **live** young.

Snakes, alligators, geckos and turtles are all examples of reptiles.

Pit viper

American alligator

Tokay gecko

Green sea turtle

Reptiles that live in water swim to the **surface** to breathe air. While they are swimming underwater, they hold their breath. Some reptiles can hold their breath for several hours underwater.

Crocodiles have nostrils on top of their snout. This means that they can breathe while the rest of their body is underwater.

Sea snakes spend all their time in the water, but they come to the surface to breathe air. Which oceans do sea snakes live in?

Crocodiles can't stick their tongues out, but alligators can! A piece of skin connects a crocodile's tongue to the top of its mouth.

SCALES AND SHELLS

Reptiles are covered in hard, dry scales to keep them safe from **predators** and sharp rocks and branches. As they grow, reptiles lose their scales and grow new ones in their place.

The scales on this snake lie on top of each other, like tiles on the roof of a house.

Crocodile and alligator scales lie flat in rows.

Tortoises and turtles have shells on their backs. Their shells are made of bones, covered in a hard smooth material, which is similar to scales. When tortoises and turtles are in danger, they pull their heads and legs back inside their shells.

Every type of tortoise and turtle has a different pattern on its shell. How did this leopard tortoise get its name?

FACT CAT FACT

Tortoises and turtles can feel when something touches their shell.

DIET

Most reptiles are **carnivores**. They hunt and eat other animals, such as insects, fish and small **mammals**, for food. Carnivorous reptiles often have large teeth and sharp claws to help them catch their **prey**.

Chameleons quickly **extend** their long sticky tongues to catch insects.

Iguanas spend most of their time high in rainforest trees, where they can find plenty of leaves and flowers to eat.

Some reptiles, such as iguanas, are **herbivores**. They only eat plants. Other reptiles, such as box turtles, are **omnivorous**. They eat fish and frogs, as well as leaves and flowers.

FACT CAT FACT

Snakes don't chew their prey. They swallow their food whole, even if it's very large. Snakes can swallow whole deer, kangaroos and even cows. How do boa constrictor snakes kill their prey?

YOUNG

Female reptiles lay eggs in nests. Some female reptiles stay with their eggs, and others leave their eggs to hatch on their own.

Female Burmese pythons stay with their eggs until they hatch. They wrap their bodies around their eggs to keep them warm.

When the young are ready to hatch, they break out of their eggs. Many reptiles are born ready to find their own food and **shelter**. Their parents don't look after them.

Some reptiles are born with a sharp egg tooth, which they use to break through the shell of their egg as they hatch. After a few months, their egg tooth falls out.

When loggerhead sea turtles are born, they leave their nests in the sand and go into the ocean to find food. Why is it dangerous for young loggerhead turtles on the sand?

MOVEMENT

Most reptiles walk and run on four legs. Some reptiles, such as lizards and crocodiles, have tails, which help them to **balance**. Chameleons can hold on to branches with their tails.

Geckos have sticky feet, which help them to climb tree trunks without falling off.

FACT CAT FACT

Some lizards lose their tails on purpose when they are in danger. This helps them run away faster and confuse predators. Their tail will grow back later. Which other reptiles can lose their tails?

Snakes don't have any legs. They use their **muscles** and scales to push themselves forward and **slither** across the ground. Their bodies make a wavy shape as they move.

Snakes climb by wrapping themselves around tree branches and pushing themselves forward.

SENSES

Reptiles find out about the world around them using the senses of sight, sound, smell, taste and touch. Some reptiles, such as lizards, have a good sense of hearing. Others, such as snakes, sense movement in the ground instead of hearing sound.

A python uses its tongue and nose to smell. Pythons can also taste with their tongue.

Most reptiles have good eyesight. They can see well from far away and recognise different colours. This helps them to find prey and stay away from brightly coloured **poisonous** animals.

Chameleons can move their eyes in different directions at the same time.

FACT CAT **FACT**

Iguanas and tuataras have a third eye on top of their heads! However, their third eye can't see – it just senses how sunny the weather is. Which country do tuataras come from?

STRANGE REPTILES

Green basilisks live in trees near lakes and rivers in the rainforests of Central America. When a predator is near, basilisks jump into the water and run across the surface to escape.

A green basilisk's long toes and fast speed stop it sinking into the water.

Galápagos tortoises live for a long time, much longer than humans! Most live for at least 100 years. The oldest Galápagos tortoise was 152 years old, while the oldest human only lived to be 122 years old.

Galápagos tortoises are also the biggest tortoises on Earth. Some weigh as much as 250 kilograms - the same weight as a pig!

FACT CAT FACT

Galápagos tortoises can live for a year without eating or drinking! Are Galápagos tortoises carnivores, herbivores or omnivores?

QUIZ

Try to answer the questions below. Look back through the book to help you. Check your answers on page 24.

1 Reptiles are cold-blooded. True or not true?

a) true

b) not true

2 Which of these reptiles has a shell?

a) crocodile

b) turtle

c) chameleon

3 Which type of animal only eats plants?

a) carnivore

b) herbivore

c) omnivore

4 Most young reptiles hatch from eggs. True or not true?

a) true

b) not true

5 Most reptiles have bad eyesight. True or not true?

a) true

b) not true

6 Where do green basilisks live?

a) in the ocean

b) in the desert

c) in trees

GLOSSARY

balance to be in a steady position where you will not fall

carnivore an animal that only eats meat

cold-blooded describes an animal whose body temperature depends on the temperature of their surroundings

continent one of the seven main areas of land on Earth, such as Africa

extend to stretch out to full length

extinct describes something that lived on Earth in the past, but does not exist anymore

female describes a reptile that can lay eggs, from which young will hatch

fur hair that covers some mammals

habitat the area where a plant or an animal lives

herbivore an animal that only eats plants

live describes something that is alive

lung a part of the body that is used for breathing

mammal a type of animal with fur that gives birth to live young

million one thousand thousand (1,000,000)

muscles parts of the body which help animals to move

omnivore an animal that eats plants and meat

oxygen a gas in the air that animals need to breathe to live

poisonous describes something that can hurt or kill you if you eat or touch it

predator an animal that kills and eats other animals

prey an animal that is killed and eaten by other animals

scales small pieces of hard skin that cover the bodies of reptiles and fish

shelter a safe place

slither to move by twisting your body

snout the long nose of an animal

surface the top part of something

swamp an area of very wet land

INDEX

breathing 8–9

carnivores 12

diet 5, 7, 12–13, 15
dinosaurs 5

eggs 4, 7, 14, 15

habitats 6–7

herbivores 13

movement 16–17, 18

omnivores 13

predators 10, 16, 20
prey 12, 13, 19

scales 4, 10, 11, 17
senses 18–19
shells 11

strange reptiles 20–21

tails 16

water 7, 9, 15, 20

young 4, 15

ANSWERS

Pages 4–21

Page 5: Other animals, such as deer and water buffalo

Page 6: Some European reptiles include geckos and slow-worms.

Page 9: The Indian Ocean and the Pacific Ocean

Page 11: The pattern on its shell looks like the pattern of a leopard's fur.

Page 13: By squeezing them.

Page 15: Because it is easy for predators to see and catch them.

Page 16: Geckos and tuataras

Page 19: New Zealand

Page 21: Herbivores

Quiz answers

1   true

2   b - turtle

3   b- herbivore

4   true

5   not true – most reptiles have good eyesight.

6   c - in trees

OTHER TITLES IN THE FACT CAT SERIES...

Space

The Earth 978 0 7502 8220 8
The Moon 978 0 7502 8221 5
The Planets 978 0 7502 8222 2
The Sun 978 0 7502 8223 9

United Kingdom

England 978 0 7502 8927 6
Northern Ireland 978 0 7502 8942 9
Scotland 978 0 7502 8928 3
Wales 978 0 7502 8943 6

Countries

Brazil 978 0 7502 8213 0
France 978 0 7502 8212 3
Ghana 978 0 7502 8215 4
Italy 978 0 7502 8214 7

History

Neil Armstrong 978 0 7502 9040 1
Amelia Earhart 978 0 7502 9034 0
Christopher Columbus 978 0 7502 9031 9
The Wright Brothers 978 0 7502 9037 1

Habitats

Ocean 978 0 7502 8218 5
Rainforest 978 0 7502 8219 2
Seashore 978 0 7502 8216 1
Woodland 978 0 7502 8217 8

Geography

Continents 978 0 7502 9025 8
The Equator 978 0 7502 9019 7
The Poles 978 0 7502 9022 7
Seas and Oceans 978 0 7502 9028 9

Early Britons

Anglo-Saxons 978 0 7502 9579 6
Roman Britain 978 0 7502 9582 6
Stone Age to Iron Age 978 0 7502 9580 2
Vikings 978 0 7502 9581 9

WAYLAND
www.waylandbooks.co.uk